INTO THE END ZONE

ROBERT DARDEN

THOMAS NELSON PUBLISHERS
Nashville

434

Published in Nashville, Tennessee, by Thomas Nelson, Inc. and distributed in Canada by Lawson Falle, Ltd., Cambridge, Ontario.

Printed in the United States of America.

Scripture quotations are from THE NEW KING JAMES VERSION of the Bible. Copyright $CR 1979, 1980, 1982, Thomas Nelson, Inc., Publishers.

Library of Congress Cataloging-in-Publication Data

Into the end zone / [compiled by] Robert Darden.
     p.   cm.
   Summary: Twenty-two professional football players describe their acceptance of Christ in their lives as the central force.
   ISBN 0-8407-7761-2
   1. Football players—United States—Biography—Juvenile literature. [1. Christian life—Biography. 2. Football players.]
I. Darden, Robert F.
GV939.A1I58 1989
796.332 '092 '2—dc19
[B]

1 2 3 4 5 6 — 92 91 90 89

To my wife, Mary Landon Darden,
with whom every day is Super Bowl Sunday.

CONTENTS

Acknowledgments

Dave Bratton, Col. and Mrs. R. F. Darden, Jr., Robert Van Darden, Kim Gorum, Chris Hansen, Jerry Hill, Bonnie Hoge, Tip Killingsworth, John Kline, Mr. and Mrs. George Landon, Don Meredith, Ed Mooney, Melinda Morrison, Steve Newman, Scott Oppliger, Tom Petersburg, Fred Raines, Grant Teaff, and John Werner.

Thanks also to the publicists and promotions directors of each of the National Football League teams represented here for providing the photographs of the players.

GORDON BANKS
Dallas Cowboys/Wide Receiver

"The Lord gave me the ability and talent to play professional football."

I was graduated from Stanford University in 1980 and was drafted by the New Orleans Saints. I spent two years there, then played for three years with the Oakland Invaders of the United States Football League (USFL). With the Invaders I was the all-time leading receiver in the USFL, and I was the only player who caught a pass in every USFL game. I joined the Dallas Cowboys in 1985.

I came from a Christian home in Los Angeles, so there really wasn't much of a choice in my lifestyle. I always believed Jesus Christ was the Son of God. I can't remember a time when I didn't believe it.

By my senior year at Stanford I was still a Christian, but I was leading my own life, which meant partying and carrying on. I thought as long as I went to church on Sunday I was O.K. But that year the Lord got tired of my lifestyle.

You see, I was miserable at the time. I was in the world rankings in the 100 meters; I had a 3.3 GPA; I was set to go to the NFL; I was surrounded by pretty girls. And I was miserable. I was losing the joy of my salvation, and my prayers were not being answered. I knew I needed to change my life. So I made a deal to study the Lord's Word. I felt the change immediately. And He's enriched my life ever since.

My faith definitely impacts what I do on the field. Colossians 3:23 says, "And whatever you do, do it heartily, as to the Lord and not to men." The Lord gave me the

Dallas Cowboys Weekly

ability and the talent to play professional football. I play as hard as I can so that He can derive glory from it. Sometimes I get tired and know I can satisfy people— but not God. The Lord has designs over your life and mine. I want to do everything I can to make those designs come to pass.

You know, it is not your responsibility to meet your desires or needs. In Mark 11:24 Jesus says, "Therefore I say to you, whatever things you ask when you pray, believe that you receive them, and you shall have them." That's God's way. I'm not required to do anything but be faithful to Jesus Christ, to do the best I can do, and to be godly about it—on the playing field or at home. He placed me on the field, not man, not my own gifts. If you do your best for Him, the rest takes care of itself.

There are three things I advise young players who want to be successful. First, you have to get right with God. He has to be first in your life. Do that and you'll have success in your life.

Second, after you are on God's team and Jesus Christ is your personal Savior, you have to do the best you can do. There is no excuse for being a great athlete and not a great student. If you spend three hours on the athletic field practicing, you can spend three hours studying. The same thing holds for a professional athlete. There is no excuse not to put the same amount of time and dedication you put on the football field as you put into being a good father, husband, friend, or brother. Dedicate everything you do to God.

Third, we need to be accountable, to love one another, to be accountable to our neighbors, to our teammates. We are called to help everyone who is hurting. Christ told us that they'll only know us by how we love one another. He gives you love, mercy, grace, and power. First Corinthians 13:2 tells us that even if we have faith to move mountains, if we don't have love, we are nothing. Love is a tremendous quality to have. If you have love, everything else is a piece of cake. Finances, health, success—that's easy money. God provides all of that for you. There is nothing He hasn't provided you if you are faithful.

PAUL COFFMAN
New Orleans Saints/Tight End

"I knew if God wanted me to play, He'd create the opportunity."

I was graduated from Kansas State University in the spring of 1978. I hoped to be drafted, but I wasn't. I got a try-out because of my roommate, Gary Spani, who was drafted in the third round. A lot of scouts looked at him, and some got a look at me as well. I heard from Green Bay and Denver. The Broncos wanted me to try out as a linebacker; the Packers wanted me at tight end. When I got to Green Bay, I was number seven of seven on the depth chart at tight end, and the Packers were only going to keep two tight ends! I went to practice each day knowing it could be my last. The last day of camp, the club cut everybody else but the starter and me. I played on the special teams that first year and didn't catch a single pass. But I had a great off-season, put on a lot of weight, and won the starting job. I did pretty well that year, catching 56 passes.

Although I had a lot of individual success with Green Bay, catching about 50 passes each year, the team never did too well. I did make it to the Pro Bowl in 1982, 1983, and 1984. But in 1986 the Packers released me. Living in Kansas City in the off-season, I got to know the Chiefs' front office people, so I called them. I spent two years on the Kansas City special teams. Then, in the summer of 1988, I signed with the New Orleans' Saints. I wasn't worried: I knew if God wanted me to play, He'd create the opportunity.

For a time the whole pro scene was a highlight; just being there was a highlight. But now that I've found

Vernon J. Biever

Christ and have a family, everything else seems irrelevant.

I first accepted Christ in 1974 for the sole reason that I didn't want to go to hell! I was in a Bible study at Kansas State. But even though I accepted Him then, I didn't take it any further. After I made the initial decision, I kind of fell back for the next ten years. So I was plenty convicted when the Word finally caught up with me!

I was a self-made man, or so I thought. I had made it as a walk-on in college and a free agent in the pros, and I had the feeling that I could do anything.

I began to date the girl who would later become my wife. (We got married in 1985.) She was a Christian, and we were attending a couples' Bible study when I really got to know the Word. Because of the study, and with my wife's help, I accepted Jesus Christ as my personal Savior. When I began to read the Word, I felt a lot of guilt. I knew the way I was living wasn't right, and I realized that I had to dedicate myself to the Lord. I've tried to do that ever since. Like everyone else, I have my ups and downs as Satan comes against me. But we go to a Bible-teaching church in Kansas City and that helps. I'm occasionally still tempted, but I've never thought for a moment that I'd go back to the way I was.

If I have any advice for you, it is don't serve professional football or make it your god. Do the best you can, but you'll be guilty of idolatry if the game or the fame or the money becomes your consuming passion. A lot of players get caught up in it.

If you do play football, do the best job you can, even if you don't make it to the Super Bowl. A football career ends quickly. When Green Bay cut me after three Pro Bowls, I had to laugh. God used that experience to show me how easily the rug could be pulled out from under you. Your next play could be your last. Just a conflict of personalities with the coach and you are gone. You can't put your faith in the things of this world.

MARK KELSO
Buffalo Bills/Free Safety

"I would have to say the highlight of my career has been the people."

I went to William & Mary College and did pretty well in football. I started all four years and even made the Academic All-American team two years. We didn't have a great team record, even for a I–AA college, but I was fortunate enough to set school records for interceptions and career tackles.

I was graduated in 1985 and was drafted in the tenth round by the Philadelphia Eagles, which gave me a pretty good feeling coming from such a small school. It was a good introduction to pro football. Also, the woman who is now my wife, but whom I was just dating at the time, lived just two hours from Philadelphia. I had a good experience with the Eagles. Philadelphia had good coaching and a good Fellowship of Christian Athletes program. I never played there though. They cut me after the exhibition season, and I signed at the end of 1985 with the Buffalo Bills.

As I go into my third year with the Bills, I would have to say the highlight of my career has been the people. Steve Freeman, who played several years with the Bills, was a great person and a great influence. Eugene Marve, who was traded to Tampa Bay, has been another wonderful influence in my life. And then there was Jerry Butler, who was one of the spiritual leaders when I got here. He influenced my life through his example, his work with the chapel program, and his concern with everything related to the chapel program.

I come from a Catholic family, and our family life was

Robert L. Smith

basically good. My parents saw to it that I attended church—my mom always got us there on time! But we were primarily Catholic, not Christian. I didn't understand the difference until college. Still, I had the benefit of a strong religious background.

My Christian testimony is more of an evolution than anything else. Although I always attended church while growing up, I never really thought of anything other than sports. One day our twenty-six-year-old pastor set up a weight room in the basement and opened it up to us. That really influenced us. We attended church regularly during high school to get to use that weight room!

I didn't have a personal relationship with God, however, until I went to college. I can't point to a day or an event when it began; it was just a gradual sort of thing. We had a strong Fellowship of Christian Athletes at William & Mary. Chris Gleason, our Fellowship of Christian Athletes leader and now an officer in the Army, was a positive influence on me. A great athlete, he encountered some misfortune on the playing field and was never able to realize his athletic potential. While that same situation hasn't happened to me, Chris taught me how to deal with the spiritual side of life. My roommate, Dave McDowell, was a senior from Pittsburgh and we became fast friends through the Fellowship of Christian Athletes. He helped me keep growing in Christ.

If you want to be a winning ballplayer, I believe you have to be whole both spiritually and mentally. I draw from my own experience here. If you're not a good athlete, you're not going to make it. You have to be physically sound. However, if you are physically sound but have the wrong mental outlook, you're still not going to make it! You have to center your life around Christ to be happy. I want Him to be the center of my life. I don't think I would have been this successful if He hadn't made me strong.

JOHN ANDERSON
Green Bay Packers/Punter

"I broke my arm three times my first three years in the league!"

I was drafted out of the University of Michigan by the Green Bay Packers in 1978. The Packers had two picks in the first round, and I was their second pick, which made me twenty-sixth overall in the draft. I've been playing for Green Bay ever since.

Now, ten years later, no one person, play, game, or season stands out in my memory. In 1982 we went to the playoffs for the only time in my career. That was the best season from a team standpoint and I guess the most memorable, most exciting time. Of course, that's one of the nice things about sports—each year everyone is optimistic. That's what keeps you young and going.

My parents were churchgoers, but I didn't make a commitment to Jesus Christ until my freshman year at Michigan. I had just made the team as a punter. At Michigan we had chapel services before each home game. I figured I should go, being new on the team. It was there that for the first time I heard about having a personal relationship with Jesus Christ.

A man named Darrell Heide worked with Christian athletes at Michigan. After the chapel service, Darrell asked me what I had thought about it. When I told him I thought it was pretty good, he asked if I was interested in knowing more about Jesus, and I told him I was.

The process wasn't a two-minute or overnight thing. It took about six weeks. Darrell told me how Jesus died on the cross for my sins and how He rose again. I took the message very seriously, but I had two problems that I

23

Vernon J. Biever

had to deal with. For one thing, my father had recently died in a bizarre accident, and I had some bitterness that needed to be resolved. Second, I felt that I'd been a pretty good guy the previous eighteen years. I'd gone to church, and though my prayer life wasn't where I wanted it to be, I was not willing to admit I'd been a bad guy. But I struggled with the message and began to read the Word.

Finally, I read Romans 8:28: "And we know that all things work together for good to those who love God, to those who are the called according to His purpose." It helped me realize that we never have had and never will have all of the answers.

I finally reached the point that I believed God knows best. Then one day, in the Student Union in Ann Arbor, someone asked me, "Do you have Christ in your life?" And I accepted Him. It wasn't a radical conversion experience. I wasn't on drugs or anything, but I knew my attitudes and priorities needed to change.

If you want to play ball, I say great! Go for it! But don't neglect your studies. Don't establish the wrong kind of goals. I'd say your chances of making the NFL are one in ten thousand. I don't say that to discourage anyone but to emphasize that your *striving* for excellence is as important as the excellence itself. It takes a lot of work and sacrifice.

Secondly, don't put all of your eggs in one basket. Develop more than one sport. During junior high and high school, you go through a number of physical changes. If you play a sport at an earlier age, it is easier than learning it later. Football is a fragile career; realistically it can be over in a minute. I broke my arm three times my first three years in the league. If your main desire is to play football, it can be taken away in a hurry. You better have something else to go on to do.

PETE METZELAARS
Buffalo Bills/Tight End

*"I caught 7 passes for 120 yards and 2
TDs. . . . That set the tone for the whole year."*

I was drafted in 1982 from "tiny Wabash College," as
they say on TV, 850 students strong. I still have no idea
how the scouts heard of me. They started coming
around my junior year and came a lot my senior year.
Then, in the third round, I was drafted by the Seattle
Seahawks.

I did all right my first year, becoming a part-time
starter. But my second year our new coach, Chuck
Knox, brought in a veteran tight end, Charlie Young.
Charlie had been around for ten years, so he became
the starter. I was his back-up, especially in two tight-end
situations. I got to play some but never as much as I
wanted. We were in the playoffs two straight years. My
third year, I had a knee injury and had to have two oper-
ations, which kept me out of play for nine weeks. The
team had a good year though, with a record of 12–4. At
the close of the season, we played for the American
Football Conference championship.

When training camp came the next year, I was looking
forward to the season, but I was traded to the Bills, who
were coming off a 2–14 year. I came in and the team had
another 2–14 season. I started with the Bills for about
half the year until the coaches made some changes in
the offense. I happened to be one of the changes. For
the rest of the year, I got to sit on the bench, stewing and
getting cold!

In 1986, not knowing what to expect, I came into
camp and went to work. Thank God, I had my best year

ever. I caught 49 balls for 4 touchdowns, which set a Buffalo record for receptions by tight ends. In 1987, although I started throughout the season, I missed four games because of an injury. It was disappointing; I only had 28 catches and didn't score at all. I'd hoped to build on the previous year and play that much better. Fortunately, this year is another season.

A couple of things stick out in my memory. I caught Jim Kelly's first regular-season pass on the first play of his first game with the Bills. We were playing Tampa Bay. I caught 7 passes for 120 yards and 2 touchdowns that day. That set the tone for the whole year.

I also remember a game when I was with Seattle. We were in the playoffs at Miami with a 9–7 record. We'd only gotten in as a wildcard team, and nobody expected us to do anything. I played the whole game because we used a lot of two and three tight-end formations. I had a great game blocking, and we controlled the line of scrimmage. In the end, we beat them. It was just amazing. They took the lead with a minute and a half left, but we took the ball back and scored. The feeling was exhilarating because nobody in his right mind ever expected us to beat Miami.

While I was injured with the Seahawks, my younger brother died of cancer. Then I got traded to Buffalo where I was benched. A lot had happened to me in a two-year period, which caused me to look for something more in life to stand with and lean on than football.

I come from a Catholic family, and I went to a Catholic school and attended Mass throughout my adolescent years. Growing up Catholic, I always knew about God, but He wasn't an important part of my life. I would go to church on Sunday and that was about it. I didn't think about God the rest of the week.

In Seattle there were some wonderful Christians, including Steve Largent, Charlie Young, Jim Zorn, and Dave Brown. When I got to Buffalo, some of the Christian guys like John Kidd and Frank Reich, the back-up quarterback, invited me to a Bible study. I knew I needed something, so I started going, and each time I learned more and more about the Christian life.

The following year I went to a Pro Athletes Outreach Conference, where I learned how God and Christ could be involved in your life every day. There at the conference I decided I wanted to have a personal relationship with Jesus Christ, to have Him involved in my life, to have Him with me all the time.

What kind of advice would I give a young person waiting to talk to me in the snow after a game? Get a set of golf clubs. No, not really! When I speak to groups, I tell folks to play every sport they can. You'll become a more well-rounded athlete and excel at a greater level. Who knows? You might get into something fantastic if you haven't locked yourself into one sport. I know several 6'4", 250-pound basketball players who decided young that's what they'd do. They never gave themselves the opportunity to play football. Play as many sports as you can. That will help you know more about your body, help you control it better, give you better footspeed and quickness, and just make you a better athlete.

BILL KENNEY
Kansas City Chiefs/Quarterback

*"Finally, in my thirtieth game, I started. . . .
I'll never forget that game."*

I'm from a large family—we had eight kids—and football was a big part of it. My father played football with the San Francisco 49ers until 1947. And I had two older brothers who both pushed me toward football.

All through high school I played quarterback and then started out as a quarterback at Arizona State. But I was red-shirted in my sophomore year and decided to leave school when the coach told me he wanted me to become a tight end. I transferred to Saddleback Junior College in Southern California for one year. The week before my first game, I broke my thumb on a lineman's helmet. The next year I transferred to Northern Colorado; they turned me into a tight end too! Fortunately, after three games, they moved me back to quarterback. Just as I was going good, I broke my hand in practice—on another helmet!

I wasn't drafted until the twelfth round by the Miami Dolphins. I was number 333 out of 334 players picked in the 1978 draft. Three weeks into training camp I was traded to the Washington Redskins. Three weeks later they cut me as well.

After that I went back to Colorado and became licensed to be a stockbroker. When the NFL season ended, I tried out with a few teams and finally signed as a free agent with the Kansas City Chiefs. Since I wasn't a top draft pick, I went the next 29 games without ever setting foot on the field: 16 straight games the first year, 13 more the next year!

31

Finally, in my thirtieth game, I started against Denver. I'll never forget that game. We beat the Broncos 31 to 14. I was 12 for 18 passing with 2 touchdowns and 1 interception; at one point I completed 10 passes in a row. The next week we narrowly lost to the Pittsburgh Steelers in the fourth quarter in the snow. Finally we beat the Baltimore Colts in the final game of the season. I threw for 3 touchdowns and 300 yards. That's how my career started.

After starting the first 13 games the next year, I was bumped to the bench by Steve Fuller, who was a high draft choice by the Chiefs. The next year, 1982, I started the first three games. Then there was a strike. I started the final three games. In 1983, under a new coach, I went to the Pro Bowl. That same year I became only the fourth quarterback to throw for more than four thousand yards—the fifth highest total in NFL history until Dan Marino came along!

It's been a roller coaster since then. I broke my thumb—the other one—in 1984 and missed six games. Even so, it was a pretty good year. The next year was also a fair year, but I was hurt again and missed the last five games. Since 1986 I've battled Todd Blackledge for the starting job with the Chiefs. I sat on the bench for the first six games in 1986 before starting again. And in 1987 I was named the starter again after being on the bench the first two games of the season. At the end of the 1987 season, Todd, who is a good Christian brother, incidentally, was traded to the Steelers.

Despite the up-and-down nature of my career, there have been some definite highlights. Currently, for instance, I'm seventeenth on the NFL all-time passing yardage list. But what I remember most is that first game I started against Denver. That was when I first experienced the hand of God. Coming in at halftime with a big lead, I went into the training room just gasping for air with cracked ribs. Suddenly, I felt the presence of the Lord like a cloud on me. Three times it touched me and lifted. I cried with joy, not pain.

I am the son of Catholic parents who divorced when I was sixteen. I sort of fell away from the church. But that paved the way for me to become a Christian on March

29, 1978, when I was a senior in college. I went to a Bible study with my girlfriend, Sandi, who later became my wife. We'd been going out for two years. She was a Christian and had decided to commit her life to Jesus when she was just fourteen. In college she felt that she needed to get back to following Jesus Christ.

I didn't want to go to the Bible study; I went for Sandi's sake. I certainly wasn't a Christian. When people asked me why I was going, I'd say I thought it was neat to sit in the back of the room and mock them. They'd say I probably shouldn't go for that reason and I'd say, "I'll go if I want to!"

I remember vividly what happened that day. Sandi and I had had all kinds of trouble. It was my senior year, and I had no idea what I was going to do. I had no home to go to; for the past five years I'd been away from what little home I'd had. And, though I had seven brothers and sisters, they were all spread out, and I didn't feel close enough to any of them to move in with them at the time. Then I went to this Bible study and people kept asking me why I was going.

Suddenly, I blurted out, "Because I need something!" I got down on my knees and began to bawl like a baby. That's what got me into the fold.

Since then, I've had my ups and downs. I was drafted, traded, and cut. After I was cut, I looked up at heaven and said sarcastically, "Gee, thanks, God!" But looking back, I've seen God's hand everywhere. It was His will that brought me to Kansas City, that brought me to the Pentecostal Full Gospel Church we now attend.

Sandi and I got back together just a couple of days before I signed as a free agent with Kansas City. We started going to church together, finding other Christians, and attending things like the Pro Athletes Outreach. We started growing in Christ together.

At Kansas City, I met my friend Charlie Getty, who led the Bible Study for the Chiefs. When he was traded, he said, "Well, Bill, it's all yours." I took that on the same year I went to the Pro Bowl. There also happened to be a tremendous growth in the number of Christians who joined the Chiefs. That's because God ordained it.

God sent me to Kansas City. Football was just a way to get here. I'll play football until God tells me what else He wants me to do. It's just a waiting game. We're doing what we're doing until we're doing what we're *supposed* to be doing!

God has shown me the reality of Himself. I have a platform to preach. I put my faith behind God and godly men and godly decisions. When I did that, I realized I had to make public my pro-life and anti-pornography stands. That's not a lot to ask of a guy in my position, but you don't see a lot of that in professional sports. I've tried, and failed, many times to do His will.

When a kid asks me about playing in the NFL, I have a standard response. First, I quote him Proverbs 3:5 and 6:

> Trust in the LORD with all your
>   heart,
> And lean not on your own
>   understanding;
> In all your ways acknowledge
>   Him,
> And He shall direct your paths.

Then I quote Colossians 3:23: "And whatever you do, do it heartily, as to the Lord and not to men." That's one thing I do believe: as a Christian, you should work harder. You've *got* to have the discipline to work hard. You should strive to be the best. Then you should be kind to one another. It *is* important to get along with your teammates.

I also talk about Ecclesiastes 12:13 and 14:

Fear God, and keep His commandments,
For this is the whole duty of man.
For God shall bring every work into judgment,
Including every secret thing,
Whether it is good or whether it is evil.

And then I end with Ecclesiastes 2:10:

Whatever my eyes desired I did not keep from them,
I did not withhold my heart from any pleasure,
For my heart rejoiced in all my labor;
And this was my reward from all my labor.

The great thing I can tell them is that everything you strive for that *isn't* after God's own heart is vanity.

If God does put it into your heart to play football, you've got to put that into proper perspective. Even if you are successful as a professional football player, you've got to remember that the average career only lasts 3.2 years.

You must exercise your spiritual mind and body along with your physical body. A great athlete, whether he is a Christian or not, has a great work ethic. Christians *should* have an edge there. You should want always to be the best.

I choose to spend time with God. People always ask me if I pray before a game. I tell them I don't: My wife and I pray—not just before a game but all year long. Not just November but June and July too. My wife and I pray for the team, the players, the coaches, everybody.

JOEL PORTER
Chicago Bears/Offensive Tackle

"Suddenly I knew I could play the game."

My dad, Nathan Porter, was born in Brazil of missionary parents and lived there seventeen years before he came to the States. When I was growing up, he would play football with me, but he didn't know much about it. Still, by the time I came along, he knew enough to help me get started. He spent a lot of time with me, and though I had to learn a lot of it myself, I did learn from him to stick with it.

My high school coach, John Outlaw, in Arkadelphia, Arkansas, was like a second father to me. Coach Outlaw taught me how to relate what I learned in football to the rest of my life, to fight for what I believed. My dad taught me many of the same things, but Coach Outlaw applied them in a more practical way through football.

I had a good high school career. Our team went 31–4–1 in those three years, which was great. All my life sports came naturally to me: baseball, football, track. I always did well, which is probably one reason why I love sports!

I went to Baylor University in 1983 and stayed until 1987. My freshman year, Baylor didn't have much depth in the offensive line, so I was second team right off. I thought I'd get a lot of playing time, and by the third game I got to play. We were getting beat in the fourth quarter when I hurt my shoulder. I was red-shirted and was out the rest of the year. Then I had a bad spring and a bad start the next fall. At that point I was moved back to second team. During that time my high school coach wrote me a letter that helped me rededicate myself to football. Five games into the season, I got my starting job back. And I've started ever since.

With my redshirt freshman year, I was a four-year starter at Baylor. The person who influenced me most was F. A. Dry, the offensive line coach. He was and is a great coach and a great friend. He went out of his way to help me then, and he's still there to help me now.

We went to the Liberty Bowl and the Bluebonnet Bowl while I was at Baylor, and both were great. But the two games I remember most weren't bowl games. One game was our victory over Texas in the last game of the season. We were pretty young and not very good that year—just 4 and 6—but we beat Texas and kept them from going to the Cotton Bowl.

The game was Thanksgiving weekend, and only the team was on campus. Our season ended after that Saturday, so we went out there and just whupped them. We went nuts. Because we were beating them pretty badly, the coaches pulled the starters out late in the fourth quarter. On the bench against Texas I realized for the first time that I was playing major college ball. Suddenly, I knew I could play the game, and that shook me up.

The other game I remember was against Arkansas during my junior year. We'd already lost three games, including two in the conference: Texas A & M by one point, 31–30, in a wild game and to SMU (Southern Methodist University) on two plays. Both were that close. That knocked us out of the Cotton Bowl, even though we'd been preseason favorites. Being from Arkansas, I'd always wanted to beat the Razorbacks. They had us down at halftime 7–14, but in the fourth quarter we exploded for 17 points. We physically dominated them— just flat wore them out and controlled them the entire second half. That was the most gratifying feeling, partly because that game was during Baylor Homecoming, partly because it knocked them out of the Cotton Bowl as well.

I didn't make a public profession of faith until late during my high-school years. I knew what it took to be a Christian since my dad was a minister. I knew every-

thing I needed to know, but I just never made my choice. I guess I took it for granted because my dad was a pastor and I was always at Sunday School, church, Sunday evening services, Wednesday night prayer meetings, Royal Ambassadors, and Training Union. So the church was a great part of my life. But it wasn't until a retreat in rural Arkansas that I gave my life to Christ Jesus. I was baptized on Christmas Day. It was a meaningful time for me.

Your faith's gotta be in all parts of your life. There are times when it's hard. It's at those times I know to go to God and say, "Help me, Lord! I need your strength and support." You know, it is easy to take things for granted when you go to the largest Southern Baptist school in the world. It's so easy when you live in a Christian and Baptist atmosphere, moreso than elsewhere, to take things for granted. I don't think you can compartmentalize your life apart from your Christianity.

What's hard, especially playing football, is that it is so

emotional. There are times you've got to control your emotions and thoughts and other times when you have to play with feeling and passion. At some point you've got to draw a line so you don't go too far. It's difficult.

I was drafted in the tenth round by the Chicago Bears in 1988. I was thrilled to get drafted even at that level. Only 300 players are drafted out of the 10,000 who play college ball, so being drafted is an honor in itself. I'd been told by some of the teams I'd go higher, and it was discouraging when I didn't. But at least I've got my shot, and that's all I've ever asked for. Just what I do with it, how I take advantage of this opportunity, is up to me.

I understand there are a number of Christians with the Bears, so I look forward to being around someone special like Mike Singletary. At my first mini-camp with Chicago, I saw Mike sitting at his locker, sharing the Bible with another guy. You don't have time to think about much during camp because you're learning all the new plays. But here was Mike, between classes, taking time to share his beliefs and thoughts with someone else. Even though we're busy and so many other things seem important, we should always make time for that.

My advice to anyone who wants to play professional ball is to totally dedicate yourself to it. You've gotta say, "This is what I want to do." In college, not a day went by that I didn't do something for football: lifting weights, running, thinking about the game, studying the plays, watching the films. You have to be totally committed. It's not for everybody; it's very, very hard. Each level is more businesslike. It's no longer just a game; it is my life, my business. You have to ask yourself, "Is it worth the effort and the time?" If it is, stick with it. You can't go into it halfheartedly.

ALLEN RICE
Minnesota Vikings/Running Back

"The one play that stands out in my mind was my throwing a pass for a touchdown against the New Orleans Saints. . . ."

A lot of things stand out from my college days at Baylor University. I think I most cherish being named Outstanding Team Player during the spring workouts prior to my junior year in 1982. That was a good moment for me.

My junior year was a great year. I got to play both quarterback and running back for the team. I'd start each game at running back. Then, on third down and short, or inside the 10-yard line, I'd switch to quarterback. During one particularly good game, I played a big part when Baylor beat a nationally ranked Arkansas team at our Homecoming. Then we turned around and beat them at *their* Homecoming the next year. My senior year, we went to the Bluebonnet Bowl, and even though we didn't win, it was a lot of fun.

Since my being drafted by the Minnesota Vikings, I've been fortunate to have something good happen every year. My rookie season, I scored my first touchdown against the Los Angeles Raiders in the Coliseum. I came in for one play and scored. Later that same year, when we were getting killed by Denver, the coaches put in some rookies. I was fortunate again; my number was called on a flea-flicker and I scored. I scored a few more touchdowns my second and third years. But the biggest year was 1987. The one play that stands out in my mind was my throwing a pass for a touchdown against the New Orleans Saints in the NFC Wild Card game.

I came from a Christian home. In fact, I was named after an uncle who was a pastor. Growing up in Houston, I grew up in the church as well. Church was just something I did on Sundays. I was in the choir and everything. Being a part of all of those activities was fun. And as I got older, I began to realize what I was going to church for. My faith was ingrown in me. Sure, I drifted away at times. There were moments when I wasn't walking with the Lord. But even when I was straddling the fence, I was going to church.

Somewhere right about the middle of college, the Lord began to deal with me. He said I couldn't live that way anymore. I began to read the Word again, and some of the Scriptures, like James 1:8, jumped out at me: "A double-minded man is unstable in all his ways." That's exactly the way it was with me. There were a lot of things I wanted to do, but all of them were about to be washed away by the compromising life I was living. Another Scripture that hit me was Matthew 6:33: "But seek first the kingdom of God and His righteousness, and all these things shall be added to you."

I had to set myself aside, get away with the Word, and seek God. I knew the way the Lord wanted me to go; it was just a matter of choice. I really began to see that I needed God. The Word proved to be true, and by admitting that, I gained everything I wanted and more. I knew the total peace He talked about, and I discovered a new joy. John 16:24 says, "Until now you have asked nothing in My name. Ask, and you will receive, that your joy may be full." I may have been happy before, but my joy wasn't full. Since then, I've been growing with the Lord. As the song says, "Every day with Jesus is sweeter than the day before."

I am now ordained in the Holiness Church in Houston, where I've lived for the past three years. In the off-season, I sometimes preach. While I'm in Houston, I go to the Rock of Salvation Holiness Church. In Minneapolis, I belong to the Emmanuel Tabernacle Church of God in Christ.

My preaching is a divine calling of the Lord. Being a preacher was certainly not something I looked forward to as a youngster. My desire was to play pro ball. The

Rick A. Kolodziej

Lord blessed me to do that, but He also called me to preach. I have nothing to boast about, for I have nothing that I didn't receive from Him. At this point, He is the central figure in my life. He keeps me going. Without Him I could do nothing; without Him I would fail.

I enjoy preaching and speaking for the Lord, so when the Vikings get a request for a religious function, I get the bulk of those requests. Sometimes I get tired. That's when I have to be honest with the Lord and say, '' Lord, I'm depending on You for this one!''

When young men ask me about playing football, their questions are pretty much the same. I tell them to go for it; it can be done. But I always interject this: ''With God, all things are possible.'' The actual percentage of kids who play pro ball is pretty small, but I don't want to discourage them. I try to let them know what the chances are, but I always say, ''Go for it!''

At the same time, I tell them to get God in their lives. If you don't have football, you don't have football. But if you don't have Jesus, you don't have eternal life.

45

DOUG SMITH
Los Angeles Rams/Center

"I knew that if I did play ball,
I'd do it for the Lord."

I went to Bowling Green University in the Mid-America Conference from 1974–1978. Not much happened. Even though I was second team All Mid-American Conference one year, I wasn't even drafted. The scouts had said I might go in later rounds, and I believed them. I didn't. Fortunately, I'd become a Christian my freshman year at Bowling Green so I could handle it. The Lord had been working on me for a while, so I knew that if I did play ball, I'd do it for the Lord.

As a free agent, I had the opportunity to go to Los Angeles, Philadelphia, or Cleveland. I chose the Rams because they needed a long snapper. As it turned out, George Allen, the new head coach, brought with him from Washington a guy who had had ten years as a long snapper. That eliminated that! But that's how I started my professional career. I don't know the odds for a free agent making a team, but three of us made the club that year.

My first year in Los Angeles, I started two games. From my second year on, I was a regular. I played three different spots on the line during my second year, four different spots my third year. For the next seven years I started at center. This past season was my fourth time to be named to the Pro Bowl.

I remember one game in particular against Buffalo. I'd broken my right hand two weeks before, and in those two weeks, I learned to snap the ball with my left hand.

The trainers fitted me with a big clublike cast on my right hand to protect it.

I was up against the Bills's great nose tackle, Fred Smerlas, and I had a great game against him until he learned what to do about my club. We're taught to block at the opponent's chest, but with my club there was no surface to grab, so it would slide right up to his chin each time—pretty hard too. Contrary to popular opinion, I wasn't doing it on purpose. We had a few words, and I told him I couldn't help it.

Anonymity is probably the thing I like the most about the game. I don't mind not being in the limelight. The way it is now, I can go to places, even shopping malls, and not be hounded. At the same time, I can share my testimony, and the fact that I'm a football player makes it that much more powerful. For some reason, people in Christian circles value celebrity testimonies, even if they are not particularly strong. Some people in your local church have much more amazing testimonies. But I'm thankful the Lord can use me for this.

As a child, I belonged to a liberal Christian church, but I wasn't born again. My father is a committed Christian, but he still belongs to that church. We went to church every Sunday when I was a boy, but I think we just paid lip service to God. In fact, I used to do isometrics during church. I'd come out of church some days really pumped up—I mean I was sweating!

Three people turned me around in my spiritual walk. One was my wife Debbie. We dated when we were in high school, and one of her father's rules was that whoever went out with her had to go to church with her. I didn't know this was a rule, but I'd go just to have this good-looking girl sitting next to me.

The pastor of Debbie's church lived across the street from me, and I'd heard him preach the gospel before. I had several questions I'd ask him, and he shared the Lord with me each time. Meanwhile, Debbie kept working on me.

Then, when I went to Bowling Green, I hit it off with a guy. I'd pick him up to go to class each day just after he finished his quiet time with the Lord. The three of them

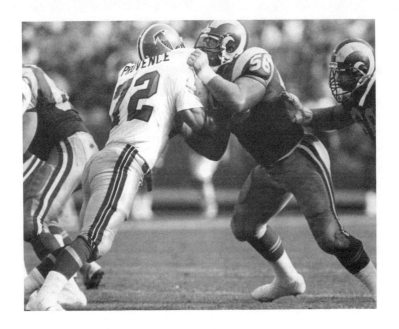

surrounded me with the gospel. Finally, a man from Campus Crusade for Christ led me to Jesus Christ in my dorm room.

Initially, I didn't take my faith anywhere. God put me through a growth process, but it has taken quite a bit longer than I wanted it to. I suppose I wanted Him to take me by the nape of my neck and *make* me a better person. I had some bad habits I couldn't defeat on my own. God has changed me over the years, and He's let me realize every day that I have to allow Him to be the Lord of my life.

One of the greatest lessons He's taught me came after a head injury I suffered about three years ago in a game against New Orleans. I got hit by Bruce Clark. Right away I experienced a numbness of my fingers. I went to the trainer, but I stayed in and played a while longer until I realized that my thoughts were slow and jumbled. The numbness traveled up my arm and my neck, into my tongue. My speech became slurred as if my tongue were fat. Almost immediately I began to experience headaches, and for the next four months, they were incredible.

As all of this was occurring, I realized that I was a football player and football players get hurt. I realized I was loving the game more than the Lord. I liked the money and the identification and the autographs—all the stuff that as a kid you think, ''That's what I want!'' I put my identity as a football player above my identity as a Christian. But in His Word, friends, God says your first identity *has* to be as a Christian. I'm a Christian who is an athlete, *not* an athlete who is a Christian. Football will end someday. I'm in my eleventh year, and my career will end shortly. My faith will give meaning to my life when football ends.

If you want to play football someday, I have to say the odds are against you. But with hard work, Lord willing, you *can* get there. I share a lot with young people about the dangers of drug abuse and the importance of continuing their education. Don't quit school. With all the computers and things we use today, you can't play the game unless you have an education. And, remember, the most important thing is that Jesus be the Lord of your life.

MIKE SINGLETARY
Chicago Bears/Middle Linebacker

*"To be honest with everyone meant . . .
getting off that white horse."*

I come from a Christian family. My dad was a minister,
and the rest of my family sang in the church choir. In
that kind of atmosphere, there doesn't seem to be much
choice in whether you become a Christian, partly because you don't know anything different.

When I got older, around 1972, I invited the Lord into
my life. My brother died in the summer of 1971, and my
mom and dad got a divorce that year. So the boy in sev-
enth grade who liked to act silly and got poor grades
suddenly found himself pushed to the forefront. It was a
trying time with so many things going on. I had to do
the right thing, things that would help instead of hinder.
Somewhere, somehow I had to start to make decisions
and make them fast.

By 1972 my life had changed for the better. It was that
summer that I decided I was going to take a stand. I
said, "I'm going to make something of my life. I'm not
going to spend my life walking the streets." I knew I had
to fulfill my duties as man of the house with my sister
and mom.

The trouble was I made a decision for Jesus for all the
wrong reasons: I wanted my mother to be proud of me,
and some guys I admired at church believed that speaking in tongues meant you had the Holy Spirit. I thought,
"Man, I gotta get it!" So I came to the Lord for all the
wrong reasons.

Ten years after that, I was not living what I was talking.
It's not that I was doing anything bad. But now I under-

stand that Christianity is not just a matter of *not* doing something. I was only measuring myself against my peers. But I was searching for the truth.

I finally realized that I was saying one thing and doing another, but I didn't want to be a hypocrite. I felt like Paul must have when he said, "Why do I do the things I know I'm not supposed to do?" I saw that my lifestyle couldn't be the way it was if I were to say I was a Christian. If you are a Christian, then walk it. If not, then get out of the way.

I picked up the Bible and read it straight through. For the first time in my life I began to understand what Christianity was. I understood how far away from the truth I'd grown. I understood that I had to live my life according to the Bible, *not* according to men. If I had a question, I learned to ask, "What does the Word of God say?" When I was faced with temptation, I'd ask, "What does the Word of God say?"

If I've learned anything, I've learned people may say they are Christians, but their fruit must be judged and not their words. Who *is* the Lord of your life? Is it you or God? Are you saying one thing and doing another? So many people are in spiritual conflict today. So many are willing to jump on the bandwagon. They say, "Yeah, it is tough to live the Christian life." But God said, "My grace is sufficient" (2 Corinthians 12:9), and "He who is in you is greater than he who is in the world" (1 John 4:4).

Although I've not said much about my professional football career, these are the events that have shaped my life. My wife has had the greatest influence on my Christian walk and is the most important person in my life. I am a different man from who I was in college. The Mike Singletary people saw at Baylor University or in high school in Houston and of whom they said, "He was a Christian . . . ," was a joke. To call oneself a Christian and then live the life I was living is religion. That's *not* Christianity.

During the first year of my marriage, I began to ask myself, "Where am I? Who is the Lord of my life? Why don't I have the authority, the strength, the faith to do the

things I know I should be doing?'' I knew the only way to find the answer was to humble myself before the Lord.

As I went before God, He said, ''If you want answers, you have to be honest with yourself, first of all; then with the people around you.'' That's the hardest thing I ever had to do. To be honest with everyone meant doing the toughest thing of all: getting off that white horse, showing everyone that Mike Singletary wasn't the perfect guy he was saying he was. But after coming through it, after I allowed myself to be broken, came the turning point of my life. I immediately received grace like I've never known.

If I were asked for advice by a young man who wanted to play pro ball, the first thing I'd say is, ''Why do you want to play?'' He'd probably give me a million reasons: the glamour, the girls, the love of it. If he said, ''For the love of it,'' I'd say, ''Great! Go for it. But make sure you understand what you're getting into.'' Football is not just a game for people who want to play at playing it. You've got to give it everything you've got.

I'd also say, "Whatever you do, make sure your grades are equal to or better than what you do on the field." If you're fortunate enough to go to college and even more fortunate to play pro ball, there's still a hole there. You're not going to play your whole life. You need something in your head to fall back on. Never forget that to excel, you have to build all areas of your life: the social, the spiritual, *and* the mental. In the end these three things are far more important than the physical part.

MIKE STENSRUD
Kansas City Chiefs/Nose Tackle

"We stopped the drive and won the game."

I spent five years at Iowa State. I was Big 8 Newcomer of the Year my freshman year, then red-shirted my sophomore year. In both my junior and senior years, I was an All-American—second team my senior year.

In 1979 Houston drafted me as the first pick in the second round. After seven years, Houston released me. I played in Minnesota for one year and Tampa Bay for one year. Kansas City recently signed me for the 1988 season.

There have been plenty of highlights in my nine years of pro ball, but the event that comes to mind first is one of the funniest things that ever happened to me. We were playing the last game of the 1980 season against Minnesota for a playoff spot. We didn't know if we had to win the game to make the playoffs. If we lost, either Pittsburgh or Cincinnati had to lose for us to make it. The game seesawed back and forth until we were up by four points at the two-minute warning. We kicked off, and they marched downfield on us in their "hurry-up" offense. I was getting winded. They were on our 30-yard line and ready to go. As their quarterback called signals, I threw up on one of the offensive lineman's shoes. When the guard instinctively recoiled and tried to wipe it off, the referee threw a flag for movement in the line and assessed them a penalty. We stopped the drive and won the ballgame. I can only laugh about it now.

I grew up in a Christian home where we were taught godly principles and godly love. Not only that, it was a home where we were in church Sunday morning and night and Wednesday evening as well. Church attendance was not a ritual; Dad and Mom loved to be there. I was taught the Bible from my infancy. I knew all about it. I knew what a relationship with Christ was. But I never accepted Him. Finally, as a freshman in high school, I gave in to the peer pressure. My Christianity wasn't from the heart, so it wasn't long before I fell by the wayside. But it wasn't my parents' fault. I saw them live their faith and love God as I grew up on our Iowa farm.

During training camp in San Angelo, Texas, the fourth year in my professional career, Mike Barber of the Oilers was instrumental in bringing me to the Lord. Strangely, the two years before, he'd really been hard on me and I hadn't cared for him. But now, I enjoyed hanging around him.

One evening we went to a movie. When we came back, some Christian businessmen were outside the dorms witnessing to students and players. One saw me and said, "Wouldn't you like to talk?" "No!" I answered. Then he asked if I was a Christian. That hit me hard. Most of the time in the past my answer had been yes. But this time my answer was "No, I'm not."

"Wouldn't you like to be?" he asked. "I *know* all about it," I told him. "I just never made that last step." That night I rededicated my life to the Lord and took that last step in following Jesus Christ as the Savior and Lord of my life.

To be honest, my spiritual life has been rocky since then. I had good fellowship with Barber that year, which goes to show that you need good fellowship. First Corinthians 15:33 says, "Do not be deceived: 'Evil company corrupts good habits.'" My mom and dad taught me that all my life. But as I moved back and forth between Lake Mills, Iowa, and Houston, I'd hang around with old friends. I thought at first I could witness for the Lord to them; they were such a good group of friends. But it wasn't long before I was back in the bars, doing the same things I'd done before.

An incident in a nightclub changed my life, however. One night it was raided and I got caught. I started to examine myself then. I was calling myself a Christian, a

soldier of the cross, and I got caught in a place like that. I realized that you had to follow Christ and not just *say* you'd follow Him. From that moment, I realized what I needed to do, but I still didn't put it into action.

About that time, I was asked to speak at a Bill Glass Prison Ministries banquet in California. Although I wasn't going to the banquet, I decided to go out and visit Mike Barber, who would be at the banquet. Mike said, "I'd like to see you, but why don't you do the banquet anyway? It'll just be five minutes. I promise." I said O.K. and flew out.

During a layover in Las Vegas, I decided I couldn't do it. I wanted to hide what had happened in Lake Mills from Mike. I didn't want him to know, so I called Mike and told him I'd missed my plane. "That's O.K." he said, " come on out anyway." When I arrived at the Orange County airport, Mike was waiting. He'd stuck around 2 1/2 hours at the airport. We went straight to the banquet, where they asked me again to give my testimony. I thought I'd just get up and try to fool them. But when I started to give my testimony, the Holy Spirit grabbed ahold of me. I couldn't go on, I had to tell them the truth. That was when I took a giant leap of faith and realized you just cannot fool God. You can fool man, but you can't fool God.

I grew during the next four years in Houston. Then the Oilers cut me, and I went to Minnesota. As a baby Christian, I was by myself. Once again I learned the truth of the verse on seeking Christian fellowship. I'm not blaming anyone in Minnesota; I needed that daily walk with the Lord, and I got away from a fellowship with other Christians. I was going back to the way I had been. My spiritual life was up and down both in Minnesota and then at Tampa Bay.

Finally, in the spring of 1988, I heard evangelist James Robison talking about relationships with Jesus Christ. At the same time, I was reading in John about falling in love with Jesus. The verse that struck me was John 5:39–40: ''You search the Scriptures, for in them you think you have eternal life; and these are they which testify of Me. But you are not willing to come to Me that you may have life.'' Jesus was talking to the Pharisees there, but He was really talking to me. Through my whole life as a Christian, I was looking through the Scriptures for arguments *for* Christianity. But I wasn't developing a relationship with Jesus Christ. Instead of finding Christ through the Scriptures, I was using Scriptures to settle arguments. In order to be successful in the Christian life, you've got to have a relationship with Christ. *That's* when the power comes. That's when God will give you the strength to overcome temptation. He will give you power in full.

My spiritual life has been good since then. Once you fall in love with Christ, you have a totally different relationship. It is *true* Christianity, I believe.

I look at so many Christians in this Norwegian community in Iowa and I'm still judgmental. I find it hard to look at people through Christlike eyes. But, when you fall in love with Jesus, you start to fall in love with people as well. James Robison talked about this at a recent conference. Once you fall in love with Jesus, your problems don't go away, but your perspective, how you handle those problems, changes. I know it has for me.

My advice to a youngster who wants to play football is to hold on to that dream. It is very difficult to make it to the pros, and the careers are short. I didn't dream of being a professional football player. My dad is a farmer, and since the second grade, I wanted to be like him. That's what I desired more than anything else. We didn't have a television until I was eleven or twelve, so I never saw football players on TV. I did like to play sports—football, basketball, baseball. I excelled at football and sort of fell into it with my size since I was so much bigger than everyone else! But I never dreamed I would play professionally.

Young people, hang on to your dream. Just have another dream too. Everybody stresses the importance of school and college. Work toward your education, not just toward your dream of playing football.

MATT CLARK
Dallas Cowboys/Wide Receiver

"Just making it through the playoffs is a big deal in Texas."

The highlight of my Corsicana high-school career came my senior year when we made the state championship game. We lost by five points, but just making it through the playoffs is a big deal in Texas. We were a 4–A high school, the second largest classification, so we got quite a bit of exposure. Before the playoffs, nobody knew who we were. Then, we kept playing well, and suddenly we were in the limelight. It didn't hit me until the night after our semifinal game at Texas Stadium in Dallas. I was home watching the news on TV when the announcer said, "All the finals are set in the state football championships." When I saw Corsicana on the screen listed in the 4–A finals, it dawned on me how far we'd come. In a small town like Corsicana, we got a lot of support; it was like we were heroes of the city.

The biggest play I can remember in my four years at Baylor University was an 88-yard touchdown run I had at Arkansas that put us up 14–0. We lost the ballgame, so the memory is a little bittersweet. But it was such a great feeling, especially while playing in Arkansas. Our fans were in one little corner of the stadium, and we had the ball down by that end zone. I caught the ball running away from that end, still hearing that giant noise that fills the stands in Arkansas, not knowing where any defender was in relationship to me. When I crossed the goal line, the whole stadium was silent. I couldn't even hear our people. I immediately looked back down the field for any officials' flags. Only then could I see our bench jumping up and down for joy.

The 1985 Liberty Bowl against LSU was another highlight of my career. No one but Baylor people gave us any chance against a 9–1–1 LSU team. They thought they'd win easily because they'd been disappointed in not getting a better bowl game or opponent. As it turned out, we dominated them, except for a runback of a punt. And even that was their second try on the punt after a penalty. I scored our first touchdown though I wasn't even supposed to be in the route. Our quarterback, Cody Carlson, got in trouble, scrambled, and threw the ball my way. I made a diving catch in the end zone. The official looking right at me didn't signal, but the other one did. We won handily. It was a good season, especially since nobody expected us to do a thing.

After the season I signed a free-agent contract with the Dallas Cowboys. Going into the NFL draft, I knew that my chances to be drafted were at best 50–50, but I was a little disappointed. I think part of the problem was that my sophomore year I was All-Southwest Conference. After that, people expected a lot of me. But the Baylor offense chooses to play quite a few receivers as a big team effort, so there are very few standouts. A lot of people who saw me as a sophomore expected me to become a big prospect. But even though my junior and senior years were good, statistically, I never had as big a year again.

The other problem with the draft was that 1988 was a big year for receivers. In the first round alone, six were taken—the most ever. So the timing didn't help. Your being a draft pick or a free agent doesn't make that much difference. I am confident the coaches are going to do their best to pick the best players possible. It simply costs you some signing money. You still have to go out and do well. Football is, after all, a business. I still have the opportunity to play and that's the big thing. A lot of players don't even get an opportunity, so I feel fortunate. I've wanted to play pro ball since I was a kid. If you never try out, you'll never know. This way if I don't make it, I'll *know* I didn't make it.

My Christian background is very strong. I can never remember not being involved in church. My father has been a deacon in our church for years. Both of my parents teach Sunday school, and my mom leads Bible studies. The most important thing my parents did for me was not tell me what was right or wrong but live as good role models. I could see them live their faith. Everyone knew where my father stood as a businessman in town. He wouldn't tell you something and do something else. My parents gave me the opportunity to learn about our faith. They never pressured me one way or the other.

I don't think you can separate one part of your life from another. You can't separate your faith from your career. What you do in one affects the other. The discipline you need for athletics is the same discipline you need in your Christian life. Discipline leads both ways.

I don't think anything happens without a purpose. And I don't think my success on the field is a coincidence. The Lord gave me the ability, good work habits, and a competitive spirit. I certainly don't think I could have achieved any of this on my own. I don't consider myself one of the greatest athletes around—the Lord has blessed me in a lot of areas. But it is important to believe in your ability.

When I have the opportunity to talk to youth groups, I often refer to Paul because of his many teaching examples that relate to athletics. Paul says, for example, that just as you must be fit for the competition so you must be fit spiritually. And your relationship with Christ should carry over into sports and your day-to-day life.

The one thing I always tell kids who want to play football is to believe in themselves. There are different levels of ability in life. I've always told people, "Don't sell yourself short!" If I had listened to people when I came out of high school, I never would have made it. They said I was too small to play college football. I came to Baylor as a quarterback, but I think all along they'd planned to switch me to wide receiver. Once there, they said I was too slow to play. I sure wouldn't have had any success if I'd listened to them.

Now I'm a free agent. I didn't get drafted—not many players in college do—but people say my chances of making the team aren't great. If I wasn't a believer in myself, if I didn't think I had the ability to overcome deficiencies, I wouldn't do it. If you think you can make it in the pros, go after it. It's more disheartening never to have tried than to sit back one day and think, "I wonder if I could have made it?" It is better to go ahead and find out for yourself. Society is negative about failure. But there are a lot of great people in history who, if they'd quit the first time, wouldn't have become great.

TOM FLICK
New York Jets/Quarterback

"The Lord allowed me to play the game . . . with a sense that I belonged in His family."

The Washington Redskins drafted me in the fourth round in 1981 out of the University of Washington. That year it was just Joe Theismann and me. I was traded at the start of my second year to the New England Patriots, where I played in both 1982 and 1983. After I was released, I signed with Cleveland and played one season. The Browns then released me, and I sat out 1985. I was signed in 1986 by San Diego and played there a year and was released. Finally, I was signed in 1987 by the New York Jets, which is where I am now.

I haven't had a glamorous career, but I have come to know the Lord through it all. Sometimes you end up on teams that have a lot of Christians; that's always a blessing. Some teams seem to have only a couple of believers, if any. I found Cleveland full of strong believers. I was tutored and helped along there by Ozzie Newsome, Tom Petersburg of the Athletes in Action, and George Lilja. Tom's like my spiritual dad. Later, I found another strong spiritual leader in Gill Byrd at San Diego. That was a great learning experience. When I came to New York, only two players were Christians, and one, Barry Bennett, who was a great blessing to be around, got traded. Now I have to stand alone for Christ. The Lord put me in a learning experience here and it is a thrilling, scary thing.

My chance to start three games for San Diego when Dan Fouts was hurt was the on-the-field highlight of my career. The game I remember best was against Denver. We were 1–8 and they were 8–1. I realized how much I relied on the Lord in those situations, especially in Denver. I never felt more at peace, more comfortable. I don't mean to imply that the Lord completes passes for you. But I knew that everything was O.K. The Lord allowed me to play the game—that's all it is, really, a game—with a sense that I belonged in His family. When you get into the situations that are on the edge—maybe your wife is pregnant or you've just been given your first nod to start—it can be a real blessing.

When I was released from New England, I wasn't a Christian. I was depressed and full of despair following a trade and a cut. From a young age, I had idolized the game of football and made it my god. A lot of players may say that. People can idolize gold and silver or property and possessions too. But I put all of my eggs in the football basket and, to that point, I'd never really taken a blow. When I was cut again I started to believe the coaches who said, "We just can't use you, Tom, you're just not good enough to play at this level."

During the off-season I was home one night when a friend asked if I wanted to go to a Bible study. I went along, mostly because I didn't have anything else to do. I had never been interested in spiritual things, except to go to church if it was convenient—to punch in the hours, so to speak.

In the middle of the Bible study the leader quoted Romans 3:23, "*All* have sinned and fallen short of the glory of God." I sat and thought about that. At first, I thought the verse was for someone else; after all, I was a pretty good guy. But the leader explained that we *all* fall short of God's standards. He explained that even society operated on the assumption that man is sinful, that people couldn't settle their own disputes but had to have lawyers and courts. He also talked about how people had different standards and different senses of failure.

Then he read John 1:12, which I later claimed as "my" verse: "But as many as received Him, to them gave He the right to become children of God, even to those who believe in His name." Then the Bible study leader said,

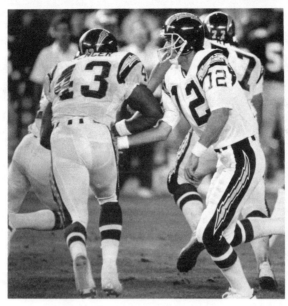

Sam Stone, San Diego Chargers

"You, just sitting in that seat"—and it seemed that he pointed right at me—"you don't have to go away. God loves you here. Now." Suddenly, I realized that God loved me even *without* a team. It was quite a release. Finally, the study leader challenged us, asking "as many as received Him," to make that commitment. I knew I had to give up my life to Christ, so that's what I did. Instantly, the pressure was off. I felt O.K. for the first time, even though I didn't have a team. Football no longer set my standards, no longer made up my character.

In his book, *Loving God,* Chuck Colson talked about how it sometimes takes a loss of power to see things clearly. Only when Colson was in the prison cell after his conviction could he see how the world worked. For me, it wasn't until I had lost my position on a pro football team that I was able to see my need for the Lord Jesus Christ. The final blessing of all this was that, after I became a Christian, I signed with Cleveland where I got to meet all those guys who had such strong faiths.

My only advice for young players is to remember that this is simply a game, nothing more. There were seven children in my family, and we were all athletic and competitive at a young age. It was hard to keep things in perspective. So when I speak at camps, I always ask the athletes if they're having fun. That's something I think we overlook. Teenagers have so much pressure from peer groups and parents. When you start adding the undue pressure of sports excellence, you're taking away the point of the game.

Dallas Cowboy's Weekly

GARTH JAX
Dallas Cowboys/Linebacker

"How on earth did you make the Cowboys?"

I was a four-year starter at Florida State from 1982 to 1986. Although I was more or less left out of the publicity for the team, I did receive an All-American honorable mention one year. I was drafted in the eleventh round in 1986, and I've been in Dallas ever since. Of course, there have been complications during that time!

I was drafted low and was a long shot to make the Cowboys. But because I had a successful preseason as a rookie, the media and the coaches said, "You've made the team." On Labor Day, September 3, I was on Cloud Nine. That day I got a phone call to come with my playbook to meet Coach Landry. I pinched myself to see if it was a dream. When it wasn't, I went. Then Coach Landry told me I'd been cut. When you're cut as a rookie, especially when you've been doing so well, there's a real emotional let-down.

But praise God, He wasn't finished with me yet. He's not going to drop a bomb on you for no reason. God is mightier than that. And He's not a God of teasing. That's definitely Satan. I just knew in my spirit that He didn't bring me along that far to cut me loose.

When I got home, the Buffalo Bills called. They wanted to bring me up that coming Monday. But then the Cowboys asked me to come back; one of the guys had walked out of camp, and they were thinking of suspending him. I did well that weekend. The day of the first Monday night game, I told the coach, "Coach, I hate to do this to you, but if I'm not on the team, I've got to go to Buffalo today. I need to know." The coach went right to Coach Landry, came back and said, "You're on." I had a good rookie season, especially on the special teams, where I was nominated to the Pro Bowl.

Last year, my second season, the first-round pick hadn't signed, so the talk was that the Cowboys would have to let go of a linebacker and keep a defensive lineman just in case. That made me expendable. Not only was I working as an inside linebacker instead of in my natural position as an outside linebacker but I also broke my wrist. The media reported that the Cowboys would only keep five linebackers, which didn't help my position either! They did, however, keep seven linebackers, and I was one of them, despite the broken wrist. God again had His hand on me, in part, I think, so I could share my testimony with the world. Satan tries to devise all sorts of ways to keep that from happening, but God has guided the outcome.

If God weren't in my life, I wouldn't be here. My life is an example of how God can use a "no-name." People say, "Garth, you're not big enough or fast enough. How can you remain up here?" If not for God, I couldn't. I'm not the physical caliber of the other players up here. But God has divinely ordained my talents to be used for His glory.

I always think of small David, who defeated the giant in his life with a pebble. The world comes at Christians with shield, sword, and spear, and we fight back with a pebble. But we come in the name of the Lord of hosts! This has always been my testimony. I love it when people ask me, "How on earth did you make the Cowboys?" I reply, "Didn't God use a nobody to defeat a giant?" Wherever I go, I can defeat that big giant with the power of God.

I was raised in a religious family but not a Christian one. I was very much an individual, even as a child. At age four, I couldn't speak, and my family feared I was retarded. Doctors say that by the age of four or five, you've developed most of the characteristics you'll carry with you the rest of your life. This was true of me. Even then, I didn't have quality friendships. I couldn't relate to

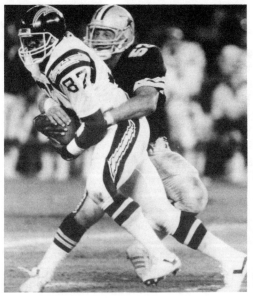

Dallas Cowboy's Weekly

anyone else, so I was by myself a lot. I never went to anyone for help. I was alone.

When I went to college, I was glad to leave the abuse I'd suffered from my family and during my high school years, but I was so empty. I tried sex, drugs, and alcohol—anything I could that I thought would give me joy or love. I never found it. I had it all, I tried it all, and I still was empty with the greatest void in my life.

But on the evening of June 21, 1985, I suddenly got on my hands and knees and prayed, "God, I don't know what You have to offer. I don't even know the purpose of Jesus Christ. But if You have anything to fill this void, I need it." I didn't know the Bible, I didn't have anyone there to teach me, and I didn't even know how to pray. I just talked. I said, "God, fill me with Your Spirit. Father, send Your Son into my life. Fill me with joy, peace, and happiness. Please." Twenty-four hours later, in that same room, I said, "O.K., God, You've convinced me." *All* of my desire for sex, drugs, rock 'n' roll, profanity,

79

and alcohol went away in the twinkling of an eye. I was *convinced*. I believe God chose me, one on one. And that was the real beginning of my life.

I take my faith everywhere. Colossians 3:17 says, "And whatever you do in word or deed, do all in the name of the Lord Jesus, giving thanks to God the Father through Him." Everything I do has to be part of my relationship with the Lord Jesus Christ, whether it is in football, school, or personal relationships. God has to be #1. Some people can separate their faith and their work; I can't. Every step I take gives me an awareness that God is prevalent in my life.

When a young man asks how he can play pro football, I offer a step-by-step process I was taught titled, "How to be Victorious." This process can be applied to your relationships with your family, your personal life, football.

The first step is to dream a dream. As a kid growing up in Houston, I dreamed I would be a Dallas Cowboy. The second step is to set goals. You can't get from dream to reality unless you set goals. The third step is to establish your priorities. That's how you achieve your goals. The fourth step is the biggie: overcome the obstacles; overcome Satan's powers of darkness.

If you've come this far, you're on the threshold. But you've got to overcome that last hurdle: persevere through persecution. A lot of people can't do it. They do the first three steps, but that last hurdle is too much. We're like gold diggers. The gold is fifty feet down. You dig and dig and dig until you've gone forty-eight and a half feet. You're that close, and you throw in the towel. The pressure is so heavy, you think, "I can't make it." Step four is always the turning point. We can't seem to push long enough.

I always tell young people that we do have the victory—we can make it. Philippians 4:13 says, "I can do all things through Christ who strengthens me." This verse promises not only that I can do great things but also that I can battle through the toughness, the persecution, and the red lights of life. Through Jesus Christ, I can work in the bad and the tough areas as well.

After sharing with young people that they *can* do the first four steps, I give them the fifth step: share everywhere the victory in your personal life and praise the Lord.

People criticize me because I talk about my previous drug and alcohol addictions. They don't like it when I tell how I was affected by the world and the problems of growing up in a divorced family. When people ask, "Garth, why do you continue to do that?" I say, "Because that's my testimony."

As an athlete, when my testimony appears, I might be the only Jesus somebody *ever* sees. I might be the only Bible someone ever reads. If that's the case, then it was all worth it. The world will come against that and people will say, "Garth, watch what you say." But if people see how I overcame my past through Jesus Christ, then they might turn to Jesus Christ for victory themselves.

GEORGE LILJA
Dallas Cowboys/Offensive Lineman

Of my four years at the University of Michigan, that last year, 1981, stands out. I was All-American and All-Big Ten at center. I was also the captain of the team at the Rose Bowl, which we won for Bo Schembechler—the only year he's won it. That was kind of neat.

I was drafted by the Los Angeles Rams in the fourth round and played there two and one half years. After I was traded to the New York Jets for a year and a half, I spent three years with the Cleveland Browns. Then I was traded to the Dallas Cowboys. My best memories are, perhaps, from my years with the only team that was a winner during that time—Cleveland. I started at left guard all three years in Cleveland. We made it through the playoffs and almost made it to the Super Bowl, until we ran into a rifle-armed John Elway.

I was blessed to come from a Christian family. My mom and dad were really strong. But it wasn't until my senior year in high school that I made a decision to follow Christ. I was brought up in Sunday school, so the terminology certainly wasn't new to me. But I finally realized what Christianity was all about. My mom and dad had laid a strong foundation for my faith to take root. And other people along the way added water to the seed.

When we finally realize the truth of the Bible, it becomes the number-one priority and affects everything else in our lives—on and off the football field, in business, in our dating lives. Christ asks us to pick up the

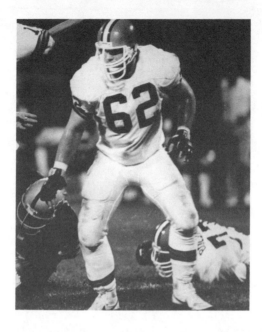

cross and follow Him *daily*. Our trouble with that is that we try to do it in our own strength.

The intensity of the sport of football is such that the more aggressive you are, the better football player you are. At a lot of speaking engagements, I am asked, "How can you be both a good Christian and a good football player?" Well, there is a line between playing hard and playing dirty. Football *is* a contact sport. The people out there realize that, and they know it is going to be rough. If you always play hard, you get their respect. At the same time, some will sense that there's something else about you that's special.

A lot of athletes feel their personal identity is tied up with being pro athletes, and they mold themselves around that. The harsh reality is that sports careers don't last forever. Football can't comfort you in hard times. As Chuck Swindoll said, the only two things that last forever are people and the Bible. You can spend time on business or at football, but that will all someday perish. But if you spend time with people and in the Word, you've made an eternal investment.

I never want to discourage anyone from dreaming about playing pro football. But I do tell people, "Never put all your eggs in one basket." If you want to play football or basketball, you should follow that dream. Play football in college if you can, but never forget your degree. If it is God's will, you'll play pro ball, and nothing will keep you from it.

Just remember this: God has bigger and better things for you to do someday. Football may seem bigger than life right now. And if it happens, if it is God's will, it will happen. But then, take that gift and give it back to Him with your testimony and your life.

Rod Hanna

DAN REEVES
Denver Broncos/Head Coach

"I thought I was the unluckiest human being in the world."

I was fortunate to be influenced by great coaches throughout my football career. During my high school years, Jimmy Hightower instilled in me the right type of ideals, character, and priorities. He influenced a lot of young people who played football at Americus (Georgia) High School. At the University of South Carolina, my coach was Marvin Bass. When I became the head coach at Denver, he was one of the first people I hired. Coach Bass was the same type of coach as Coach Hightower. He wasn't the type who screamed and hollered. He treated you like a man and expected you to respond like a man. It was my first time away from home, and he was like a father to me. Then, in professional football, I had a wonderful example in Tom Landry with the Dallas Cowboys. So I've been fortunate to be trained by three outstanding coaches, the highlight of my career so far.

Of course, prior to my football experience, my mother and father instilled in me the same types of ideals. Because I learned these truths while growing up, they stuck with me. I came from a Christian home and accepted Christ as my personal Savior at the age of nine. We attended a small country Baptist church and went to Sunday school, church, training union, Sunday-evening services, Wednesday-evening prayer meeting—everything. I was raised in a home where church activities were always available. Nothing was pushed on me, but it was offered for its own sake. I think this is some-

Rod Hanna

thing all responsible parents should do. Not all people take the time to expose their children to that. Religious faith is not something that, all of a sudden, is going to become very real. You have to choose that way of life. Every child deserves the opportunity to see it.

My faith has always been a growing experience. There is no high or low point in my life. And though things have always seemed to go the way I wanted, we *all* sin. It's a wonderful thing to know that Jesus Christ is always with us. You need a steady walk with God because you never know, particularly in this business, when you are going to need God on your side. You can be on a mountaintop one day, then the next day be lower than lows. It's great to know that Someone loves you, regardless of the situation.

As a result, my faith is with me every play of every game. I don't see how you can separate your faith and the rest of your life. Certainly there are times when you fall short and you hurt God. Certainly God doesn't enjoy being disappointed. But He loves us enough to pick us up each time. I can't separate Him from my life at work, at home, or during the game.

If you want to play football, you couldn't be shooting for anything that would be more rewarding or exciting than coaching or playing football. Dreams *can* come true if you work hard and dedicate yourself to them. The Lord has a plan for everybody. Whatever His plan for you, it will be rewarding.

I didn't think about becoming a coach until after I'd played for four years. In 1968 I injured my knee. I thought I was the unluckiest human being in the world. I thought, "God, why did You do this to me? My career's over." But He did have a plan for me. In 1970 Coach Landry asked me to become an assistant coach. That was the first time I thought about coaching. If not for that injury, my life might never have taken that turn. Of course, when I was in pain, I didn't look at it that way. You should have ideas and goals. Then, every day, ask the Lord for the wisdom and strength and courage you need. And everyday He'll give them to you.

Through it all, I've felt the hand of God. I daily ask the Lord for wisdom. And after I ask it, a thought will flash through my mind, perhaps a situation in the draft or a play on the field. Everything happens almost instantaneously, and I think, "Where in the world did *that* come from?" Or, after making a tough decision, I'll think, "It is strange that I made that decision—I never thought of that before. Gosh, the Lord really *was* there!" I don't pray for success, victory, or glory—just wisdom.

After we lost the last two Super Bowls so badly, I was as low as I could go. I asked God for peace and understanding. I don't know how I handled it as well as I did, except that I asked Him to help me and be with me. And He did. Those were not easy situations, but the Lord helped me to overcome the two toughest events in my life and to handle them courageously.

BARRY BENNETT
New York Jets/Defensive Lineman

"I really wanted to be a professional golfer."

When I finished high school, I didn't know what sport I wanted to play. Although I was the state heavyweight wrestling champ and played football, I liked golf best of all. I went to Concordia College, a Division III school in Morehead, Minnesota. It was a Lutheran college, though I'm not Lutheran. I went to Concordia for two reasons: I wasn't interested in big-time Division I schools where you play football year round. If I'd been thrown into a Division I school, with my priorities, I might have quit. I just didn't want to play spring football or have a mandatory conditioning program. Even so, I went up from 220 pounds to 260 pounds in four years.

The other reason I went to Concordia was for the head coach, Jim Christopherson. Coach Christopherson's Christian influence was important. Given the choice, I wanted to play for a Christian.

After I graduated, I was drafted by the New Orleans Saints in the third round and spent four undistinguished years at defensive tackle. The Saints' coach, "Bum" Phillips, believed you should live where you work and work where you live. But my wife and I have family roots in Minnesota, and we believed the kids should be around their grandparents and cousins. "Bum" and I disagreed, and he cut me loose. I signed with the Vikings, but they waived me just before the first game. In September of 1982, I was signed by the New York Jets. After sitting on the bench for two years, I became a starter on the defensive line, and have continued to start the last four seasons, mostly because I stayed healthy when starters like Mark Gastineau and Joe Klecko didn't.

In December 1987 I finished my tenth year in the NFL. Since the Jets didn't have too good a season, they made some changes, which affected a lot of the older players. I was traded to the Los Angeles Raiders, but they cut me loose in the summer of 1988. At that point, I came to a crossroads. Although I think I have some time left, it is tough to compete with a twenty-four-year-old kid. My health's in my favor, but age is working against me as I try to find employment for the 1988 season.

I came from a Christian background. While my folks brought me up, we attended a Baptist General Conference Church. My dad even went to Bethel College Seminary in Minnesota. We attended a small country church, where the average age of members was sixty-five, and 99 percent of the people were farmers—though we weren't. It was a good church attended by godly people.

I discovered at a young age that my parents' going to church gave me no spiritual guarantee. So one night I asked my mom to pray with me to become a Christian, even though at the time I was probably too young to understand it fully. That was step one of my walk with God. Since then I've just been trying to live a more solid Christian life. I've encountered no major pitfalls. We never kept any alcohol in the house; my parents gave me no reason to rebel against them. So, praise God, I've never taken any real digressions from my faith.

Through the years, I've felt God's hand guiding my athletic career. The strange thing is I really wanted to be a professional golfer. There aren't too many people out there who want to be professional golfers and wind up professional football players! That's happened other times in my life when I've let God call the shots. He says, "I'll call the shots, and I'll take good care of you." He told me to go to Concordia with no intention of playing pro football, but fourteen years later, here I am. For some reason, God has wanted me in athletics. A lot of guys get more "religious" when things hit rock bottom. But I've felt His presence through the successes. I'm not arrogant enough to think that I'd be anywhere without

His help. It is obvious to me that, whatever measure of success I've had, God has had a hand in it.

If you want to play football, follow the advice Jim Christopherson gave me at Concordia. I was a dominant player there, and eventually two or three scouts wandered by and asked, "Who is this number 73?" It was at that time that Coach pulled me aside and said, "If you want to play professional football, set your goals. But don't put all your marbles in one bag. Make sure that a good education is one of your options." That really fired me up because, for the first time, I believed that I had a legitimate chance to play pro ball. Coach kept my feet firmly on the ground. He said, "The odds are astronomical against your playing. But if you keep growing and stay healthy, you've got a shot." To want to play football is a noble goal, and it's very important to have goals. But there will be roadblocks along the way that you'll have no control over.

Also, as long as you're in high school, don't give up

basketball, wrestling, track, golf, or baseball to play football. Enjoy all sports. When you've graduated and the football recruiters are coming by, *then* say, "I'm a football player." It is far more beneficial to be good in a lot of sports than to go to the weight room every day by yourself. In Minnesota the biggest problem sport is hockey. Parents want their kids to be hockey players beginning at age six. And if they don't make it, they don't have anything to fall back on. Enjoy all the sports; set your goals high; have other options. Remember, only one out of 100,000 high school students makes it into professional athletics.

DAVE BROWN
Green Bay Packers/Cornerback

"Being on a winning team is always nice."

I'm now in my fourteenth year as a pro. I was a number one draft pick by the Pittsburgh Steelers in 1975 from the University of Michigan. I spent one year with the Steelers, which happened to be the year we won Super Bowl X. Then I was picked in the expansion draft by the Seattle Seahawks, where I played for eleven years. In August 1987 I was traded to Green Bay.

I've got a lot of great memories so far, but the Super Bowl year stands out. Being on a winning team is always nice. And for a rookie to come from a winning program in college and go to a winning pro team is great. You can spend your entire career trying to achieve it again. Until the end of my rookie season, I didn't realize how much work, how much togetherness goes into making a winning team.

During my first year in Seattle, I met a Seahawks linebacker named Ken Hutcherson. The thing I noticed most about "Hutch" was that he always had a smile on his face. His joy was genuine. It wasn't artificial. After observing Hutch for months, I asked him one day, "What makes you have such joy and peace?"

"It's the personal relationship I have with Jesus Christ," Hutch replied. At first I didn't believe him. But Hutch went on to tell me about Jesus Christ and God's purpose for sending Him to earth. Here was the assurance of eternal life I had been looking for, but it was almost a year later before I did anything about it. Attending a Pro Athletes Outreach conference in San Diego, I accepted Christ into my life. "Lord Jesus," I

prayed, "I need You. I ask that You come into my life to be my Savior and my Lord. I ask You to forgive me of the sins that I have committed." I then thanked Him for coming into my life. Although there wasn't any lightning when I said yes to God, I've never been the same since.

When I was young, I had dreamed of playing pro ball. The good Lord allowed this dream to come true. You may have the same dream. If so, these are the two most important things to remember. First, obey your parents. The Bible says in Ephesians 6:1–2: "Children, obey your parents in the Lord, for this is right. 'Honor your father and mother,' which is the first commandment with promise." Second, do not be deceived by bad company. Bad company can corrupt good morals. The people you hang around with can do irreparable damage to your grades and your good name. That's how most kids get involved with alcohol and drugs.

There is nothing wrong with dreaming of playing professional football. But someday soon you *must* consider what Jesus Christ means in your life. Before you do anything else, you *must* get your life right with God. Then, if it is God's will that you be a professional athlete, it will happen. But only then.

AL HARRIS
Chicago Bears/Linebacker

"I was just a typical jock."

I grew up in an air force family. Just as we'd establish ourselves somewhere, we'd have to move somewhere else. The world would consider our family moral—we didn't curse, drink, or smoke—but we weren't godly. I only heard about the Word of God from my two grand-mothers. Both shared the Lord with me when I was lit-tle, but I didn't remember that or any of the Scriptures they told me until many years later.

My self-esteem in high school came from both my family and sports. We were a close family, and I was a successful athlete. I idolized Jim Brown and Paul War-field. I was popular. I was a high school All-American at defensive end, and I turned down scholarships in bas-ketball to play football. I was just a typical jock.

Then I went away to Arizona State. It was my first time away from the nest, and, suddenly, I found that every-thing I had based my esteem on was built on sand. My family was not a permanent fixture in my life. They couldn't afford to travel from Hawaii to Arizona very of-ten.

Also, for the first time in my football career, I didn't start. We had a good team. We went 12–0 in 1975 and beat Nebraska in the Fiesta Bowl to finish the season as the number two team in the nation. My fantasy was to play in the NFL, and by my junior year, I almost got kicked off the football team for daydreaming so much about that fantasy!

Without my family, I became homesick and fell in with a group of "friends" who helped me party too much and drink too much. I'd never been a drinker before, but now I was getting drunk three times a week. Although I thought it was fun at the time, it was stupid, and I almost got killed. I had trouble in other areas as well. I became the opposite of what I was raised to be. Now when I tell people how wild I was in college, people—especially those from my high school days—don't believe me.

My senior year was my best year. I was named an All-American and appeared on Bob Hope's TV special. But I was completely in the world. People were always hanging around me, and I became lifted up with pride. Satan does that, you know, when people begin to idolize you. Of course, I loved it, but it all began to fall downhill in 1979.

I was drafted by the Chicago Bears and injured my knee the first week. I know God didn't cause that injury, but He worked through it to show me how vulnerable I was. I had a "Superman" attitude, thinking I could never get hurt. I was deceived. I put my trust in things outside of God and, as you know, those will not stand.

After missing my rookie year, I went back to school to complete my degree. It took me three spring semesters to finish. During that time the Lord began to send Christians across my path to point me in His direction. One young lady, in particular, greatly influenced me.

The first time I met her, I thought, "Hmmm." She seemed to be happy-go-lucky, kind of silly, kind of cute. Although she witnessed to me, I didn't think as much about the Lord as I did about her. She finally asked me to go to a Bible study, and because she was going, I went. At first I thought, "I don't need this!" I'd rarely gone to church before and had never seen people like those I met at that study. I was surprised. I thought perhaps they were phonies because I'd never seen someone enjoy talking about Jesus. But I soon saw that they were genuinely having fun.

I continued to see that girl. She'd witness to me, but she always kept her distance, remembering, as I later found out, the biblical injunction about being "une-

qually yoked." I didn't understand why she wouldn't date me, but she remained my friend.

God kept putting others in my path on the campus. One day God put it on one guy's heart, though he didn't know me, to walk up and talk to me about the Lord. "Do you know Jesus Christ?" he asked. "Do you want to know Him?"

"I know He was born in a manger and died on the cross. That's about all I know."

"But do you *really* know Him?" the fellow persisted. I thought he was some kind of religious nut. He followed me a good quarter of a mile home. You can imagine how hard he'd prayed to God about me. I could have clobbered him. But I didn't open my mouth. And even though I wondered then if the guy was crazy, some of the things he said stuck with me.

The next week, another guy I didn't know came to me at McDonald's and gave me a pamphlet about Jesus

Christ. By now I was *really* interested. When I finally returned to training camp for my third year with the Bears, Vince Evans and Roland Harper began to pursue me. I'd ignored them the previous two years. They would come up to me with a Bible, and I'd run away.

One night I went out with some of the guys, bar-hopping, talking worldly talk. We gossiped about other players and boasted about how good we were. But someone was praying for me that very night. Like the song "Amazing Grace" says, "I was blind, but now I see." Suddenly, in the bar, it seemed that the eyes of my spirit were opened and a veil was lifted from them. I hadn't turned to the Lord yet, but I could see the sin in my life and in the lives of the guys I was with. Most of us worshiped football.

Now I asked myself, "What is truth?" And then I said, "I'm a phony. I'm tired of living my life like this."

One week later I got a pamphlet from the girl who first started witnessing to me. It had a graph that showed God first and everything else second.

Later that day I sat impatiently waiting for lunch when Vince Evans came up and said, "Patience is the key."

"How did you know what I was thinking about?" I asked.

"Because I saw that God is working on you," he replied. "Jesus Christ will change your life. I'm not talking about religion. I'm talking about a personal relationship with Jesus. If you were the last person on earth, Jesus Christ would forgive your sins."

As he shared God's love with me, it struck me how much God did love me. Although I didn't understand how and why He loved me, I knew God was real and He did love me. But I still didn't know how you could have a personal relationship with Him—how He could be a part of your everyday life, how He cared about the little things. I'm still learning that last part. Vince told me that God loved me so much that He sent His Son to die for me and that I should love Him based on that, not on what I could get or not get from Him.

That same day in Bible study, Van Crouch shared the gospel with me. Satan immediately began to play mind games with me as I thought, "These guys are going to preach to you; they're going to judge you." But no one was judgmental. These were guys I could talk to, guys I could trust, guys who cared about me.

As Van preached from the Proverbs on the love of God, all of the Scriptures I hadn't heard since I was four came back to me. That night I got on my knees. I recognized that I was a sinner and that Jesus Christ died for me. Jesus revealed Himself to me that night, and He hasn't stopped revealing Himself since.

From my years with the Bears, I particularly remember one game against Washington in the 1984 season. The game stands out because it reminds me of the days when the Christians were persecuted in the arena with the lions. I think this game was the first time we recognized that the Bears were pretty good. We had a promising club, but no one thought we had a legitimate shot at being contenders. We played the Redskins at RFK stadium and were heavily rated underdogs. No one believed we would win, but we did. It turned out that we finished the season 10–6 and lost in the championship game to San Francisco.

I've got four things to say to someone who wants to play pro football. These are things that really helped me get here, and there are probably lots of guys on the street who are stronger and faster than I am. The first thing is: Don't listen to people who tell you you can't do it. If it is the Lord's will that you *don't* make it, you won't. Whenever you do something profitable, do it to the best of your ability. Some people will always tell you you can't. Don't listen to them. Examine their lives. Those people sit on the sidelines and watch others, hoping they'll fail. They remind me of the children of Israel coming out of Egypt. Those who didn't believe they could make it to the Holy Land died, wandering in the wilderness.

Second, be coachable. Listen to the coach. Be a team player. My coaches helped me a lot. Those coaches want to win. Listening well gets their respect.

Third, be persistent, be steady.

And fourth, don't base your identity only on sports.

Football is an emotional roller coaster. If you base your self-esteem on what the coach says or what the media say or what the fans say, you'll lose it in a hurry. But if your self-esteem is based on Jesus Christ, it'll last. Be steady. So many football players are who they are as players. When that changes, they fall to pieces. Don't base your identity on football.

RAYMOND BERRY
New England Patriots/Head Coach

*"There was one business I didn't want to
get into: I didn't want to be a coach."*

The turning point in my life was a conversation with
Don Shinnick, my best friend while I was with the Baltimore Colts. He had known me for three years, and we
had roomed together on road trips. He made the person
of Jesus Christ real to me, and through his influence I began to think in different terms. This was in 1960 during
my sixth year of professional football. I was twenty-
seven years old at the time. Through Don's influence, I
put my trust in Christ.

I was raised in a church and I believed all the historical
facts about the life of Christ. But I didn't have any idea
what Christianity was all about. When Don was talking
to me, I had to face the issues in my own mind that I
didn't have any answers to. So I was receptive to what
he had to say.

I didn't know what my purpose in life was. I'd come
to realize that my athletic ability was a gift of God—there
had to be some reason for it. But I didn't have any idea
what would happen to me if I died. I had no peace in
my life, and I was wrestling with a burden of guilt.
When I put my trust in Christ, however, I experienced
peace for the first time.

As I began to study the New Testament, I dealt with
the subject of eternity and death. I then realized the gift
of eternal life that came with one's knowing Jesus Christ.
It took about a year of studying the New Testament to
understand that, and I had a hard time believing it. I was

109

so aware of my sinful nature that I couldn't understand how a sinful man could have such assurance.

After that, things began to change gradually. I began to question why I did what I did for a living. Only later did I begin to understand that God can and does use unlikely vessels. Grown men who like to chase a silly football around are not beneath Him.

Being a Christian in sports was different back then. The movement was just beginning at that point. I didn't find any problems in it; it was just different. Watson Spoelstra, a sportswriter with a Detroit newspaper, was a tremendous influence on my wife and me. We had just gotten married, and my wife was a very young Christian. Watson had a great personal relationship with the Lord. We could see how he'd get answers when he prayed, and we imitated his example. Until then I was not aware that a person could have such an intensely personal relationship with the Lord.

Today when I look back on my career, I have a tremendous awareness that His hand was on my life. So many years in my life, I had no idea it was there. When we won our first championship game with the New York Giants, I remember being conscious that I needed to thank God for the victory. I have an overwhelming memory of the after-the-game experience. I wasn't even a Christian at the time, but I was impressed on my way to the locker room that I was to shut the doors to a side room and pray. This had been going on for two or three years as I grappled with those same questions of my purpose in life and my relationship with Jesus Christ. Now, as I look back at what happened, I see I was really searching for a reason to live, an answer to eternity, and for a means of forgiveness of sin. The answer for all three can be found in Jesus Christ.

I have felt the Lord's purpose for my life two different times. I first became a Christian during the prime of my playing career. That first year the Lord showed me in many ways His personal love for me. He very gently asked me then, "Why is it you've never asked me what I want you to do with your life?" The grace of God that brings you to be a Christian also gives you the opportu-

Jim Grange

nity to relinquish your own life and let Him take it over for you. Finally, I answered His question: "What do You want me to do? I am willing, Lord."

At that time, I thought His will meant my not playing anymore. That was a crucial experience because I think that was the last step in His process to set me free. I didn't understand that once I had surrendered my will, I would be completely set free. Until then, football had been my god—the thing I was serving and worshiping. It could have been gone in a minute. I was in chains.

Shortly after that the Lord revealed that He wanted me to continue to play. The key thing was not that He wanted me to get out but that He wanted to know if I was willing to get out for His sake.

The other experience came as my professional playing career began to wind down. I knew there was one business I didn't want to get into: I didn't want to be a coach. I had negative feelings toward the profession. I'd been around it all my life, and the public humiliation a coach goes through didn't appeal to me. Also, I felt completely inadequate to the task. But as I sought God's direction for my life, it became clear what He wanted me to do, and I knew I had to do it. Learning to trust Him in a very difficult profession has been challenging, but it has been a valuable growth experience for me.

I was a part of two different coaching staffs that got fired. When I was appointed coach of the New England Patriots, it was the middle of the season and I wasn't even in coaching at the time! The circumstances that worked to thrust me into that position were absolutely bizarre—things that wouldn't have happened in a million years without a Divine plan.

Going all the way to the Super Bowl the next year was a wonderful experience, defying any type of logic. When it was all over, *nobody* could give the glory to anybody but God.

Young people don't often ask me for advice on playing football. Of course, there's no doubt in my mind what the answer is, but most people are not ready to hear it. The greatest experience you can have in life is to have a personal relationship with the Lord. A part of having that relationship to is to obey, serve, and follow Him. You must commit yourself to what He wants you to do. That's what life is all about; that's what's fulfilling. If I paint a life picture any other way, it's not accurate. I'd like to be able to say to young people, "I'd like the best for you and the best for you is God's will. Go out and find it and do it. His way is the *only* way."

About the Author

Robert Darden is an author and journalist, the editor for The Wittenberg Door, and the gospel music editor for Billboard. Darden lives in Waco, Texas.

For Information about other Christian Sports Ministries, Contact the Following:

Athletes in Action
6264 Lehman Drive
Suite A-101
Colorado Springs, Colorado 80918

Fellowship of Christian Athletes
8701 Leeds Road
Kansas City, Missouri 64129

Institute For Athletic Perfection
P.O. Box 627
Branson, Missouri 65616

Professional Athletes Outreach
P.O. Box 1044
Issaqua, Washington 98027

Sportspower Ministries
P.O. Box 433
Lee, Massachusetts 01238